ABOUT ROOT EXPERIENCE

Root Experience is an arts charity whose purpose is to inspire people, of all ages, to positively connect with themselves and the world around them.

Whether taking interactive events to communities or running creative workshops in schools, our work is about encouraging people to see things differently.

Initially founded as a theatre company by Simon Magnus in 2008, today we use games, drama and events to help participants explore, learn and challenge with curiosity and compassion.

Hidden Stories

HiDDEN STORIES

Artistic direction by Simon Magnus
Written by Simon Magnus and Samantha Wraith
Illustrated by Tinne Luyten

Co-creators

Sharon Aprile, Tracey Bertram, Helen Brook, Tracey Ginn,
Jonathan Hammond, Caroline Hilderbrando, Kelly Keep,
Rosanna Lowe, Charlotte Meldrum, Jane Muir, Luc Raesmith,
Sarah Saeed, Thomas Silk, Mat Smith, Robert Stedman,
Jo Thompkins, Louise Tondeur, Christine Young
and four other people who wish to remain anonymous.

This book wouldn't have been possible without the tireless efforts of Rachel Cohen, Natalie Scott and Kelly Smith.

None of this would've happened if it wasn't for an incredible ITV People's Projects funding campaign ran by Emma Chapman and Jessica Cheetham.

A massive thank you to the Root Experience board of trustees and to everyone else who has supported our journey to make and publish this book.

First published 2019 by Independent Publishing Network
Printed by Instantprint
Cover design, typesetting and illustrations by studio tinne luyten
Copy-editing by Kelly Smith

The Hidden Stories book was created with support from the National Lottery Community Fund

ISBN 978-1-78972-142-3

The Hidden Stories website (www.hiddenstories.co.uk) was created with support from the Betty Messenger Charitable Foundation

CONTENTS

FOREWORD

Invisible conditions impact millions of people worldwide on a daily basis. They cover conditions as wide-ranging as diabetes, fibromyalgia, arthritis and HIV. Invisible conditions can also incorporate, exacerbate and lead to a range of issues associated with mental distress, such as depression, anxiety and agoraphobia.

People who live with these conditions experience a 'double bind,' weighed down not only by their symptoms, but also by the social implications of these. They face being disbelieved and being made to feel illegitimate. Their friendships and family relationships can suffer as they feel forced to withdraw from social engagements or cancel one too many nights out. Employment can be difficult to get and to keep; jobs are lost; careers falter. Some of these conditions, such as pernicious anaemia and ME (chronic fatigue syndrome), resist easy diagnosis, so these battles can extend to people's engagement with the healthcare system too.

I understand these tensions both from a professional perspective, as an academic interested in exploring and elucidating people's experiences of invisible conditions, and from a personal perspective, as the partner of somebody who lives with an invisible condition. These dual interests brought me, some four years ago, to the work of Root Experience. Simon asked me to observe some of the workshops and other events which Root Experience ran in the early days of this project, and I have been privileged to remain on this journey with them ever since – albeit from a very backseat position!

Over the course of this journey I have seen first-hand the power of the arts to connect with people, to transform the ways in which those who live with a wide range of invisible conditions understand their experiences, helping them to cope when they are struggling, and empowering them to speak out. On the other side of the coin, I have seen the audience of these courageous stories and artworks feel validated by hearing/seeing pieces that speak to their own experiences or be challenged into thinking differently about invisible conditions – perhaps even thinking about these for the first time.

These are voices that need to be heard, stories that come from a few but speak to so very many different people's lives. They speak of struggle, rejection, misunderstanding, bravery, resilience and, perhaps more than anything, of strength. I hope that you too will find strength in these pages, whether it be to continue to live the richest, fullest life you can, to take time to step back from the pressures crowding down on you, or to support others in reaching these aims.

Dr Helen Johnson
University of Brighton

INTRODUCTION

The journey of this book started, as so many of these things do, with something really personal. Well, maybe not so personal for me but definitely personal for my dad. You see, for the last 30 years he's lived with MS, a neurological condition that for him presents, in one way, as being unbalanced when he walks. To others, he might look like a drunken old man walking down the high street. Most people usually respond by either ignoring him, pushing past him or giving him a wide berth, making it glaringly obvious they're avoiding him. Unsurprisingly, all of these things make it harder for my dad to ask for help when he needs it.

Curiosity led me to seek out people with various conditions that aren't easily noticed by others – or are simply well hidden. I wanted to find out if they had experienced similar behaviour. I wanted to know if this kind of thing was common for all people living with something that others can't see. I asked: what is the external – and internal – stigma that people feel and how does it affect their everyday lives?

It's hard enough for people living in a system that doesn't adapt to their needs, in which they constantly have to explain their realities to get by in life. It could be asking for extra assistance in a shop, needing a seat on a bus, being overlooked for a promotion or dealing with debilitating benefit cuts. To have to deal with judgements from the outside world just adds to what is, for many, an already challenging and often isolating existence.

Worse still, I found that many people had difficulty explaining how they were feeling to friends and family. They were constantly holding back from telling the people they care about what they needed for fear of being rejected.

THE WORKSHOPS

As a theatre maker, I know how powerful the arts can be in helping people to see things differently, and to make sense of internal struggles that are almost impossible to put into words. So, in 2017 I began running creative workshops in Brighton through our arts charity Root Experience. We wanted to offer a safe, accepting space where people could explore what was going on for them under the surface and express themselves without judgement.

The people who signed up identified with all sorts of invisible conditions, from anxiety to OCD to chronic fatigue syndrome. Some called these illnesses, some disabilities and others just said it's 'a part of me people can't see'. The participants were a diverse group of individuals, all with really different lives and ways of being. But they shared two fundamental things. Firstly, a need to reveal some of their most vulnerable parts to people they barely know – just to be able to go about their lives. Secondly, the pain they feel when they're unable to reveal these parts.

The workshops, however, encouraged participants' instincts to flourish. They were creative, experimental and took on an extraordinary life of their own. Everybody in the room was a participant, including me. We found a level of freedom that enabled us to move away from the labels of diagnosis, and instead talk openly about how we experience the world, and what we share and don't share.

These workshops sparked a positive connection, inspiring courageous conversation around things that had previously brought shame for some people in the room. I began to see the potential of this work – not only in helping people to find their voice, but also in stimulating the compassion needed in others to hear and understand those voices.

So, we decided to enter ITV's The People's Projects, an initiative aimed at boosting community-based causes. Thanks to a well-supported cam-paign, we won enough funds to meet more people and create this book.

Starting in our home-town of Brighton, we took our workshops as far as our funding could stretch within the south of England. We put out an open invitation and people flocked in. From teachers and authors to support workers and those unable to work, they were all incredibly resilient individuals who shared their stories with courage and generosity, and who sought to creatively explore their relationship with the world around them.

UNEARTHING THE COMMON STORIES

After the workshops I introduced my collaborator Samantha Wraith (an artist and drama-therapist) to a huge treasure trove of material: drawings, photos, writing, recordings. We even had stacks of labels that people had written for themselves, expressing how they felt they were seen by others and how they saw themselves. Like before, the wonderful diversity of people shone through – in unique encounters, struggles and ways in which participants found support.

Yet there was much in common about their experiences and challenges, and the feelings they had about them. What was shocking, but unfortunately not surprising, was the sheer amount of emotional and psychological health issues felt by most people living with invisible conditions that, in the textbooks, have nothing to do with those conditions (or specific mental health problems). So many stories spoke of isolation and stigma and how these lead to fear, low self-esteem and loneliness.

It became apparent that we needed to honour the process we'd been through, by letting the participants' own voices sing over those of their conditions. For them to be seen and heard without being defined by what many parts of society refer to as disability.

Of course, there was no way we could even hope to represent every person we'd come into contact with, or all invisible conditions (each person will experience the same condition differently). We felt that there was a simpler, more powerful way to approach the material, and that was to let the univer-sal truths emerge and show what, deep down, makes us all human.

With that, we decided to focus on the fundamental things we learnt from participants and bring together their stories in a way that would help others relate to them (and perhaps even feel inspired to share their own stories).

So, what you'll see in Hidden Stories is a combination of many different perspectives, told through the lives of three main characters – which have been brought to life skilfully and sensitively by our brilliant illustrator Tinne Luyten.

Broadly speaking, one character lives with mental health problems, one is neurodivergent (a term for all sorts of brain-related conditions, such as autism), and one has a form of chronic pain and fatigue. However, each holds the possibility of many invisible conditions. And throughout the book, participants will recognise different parts of their contributions, and perhaps those of others in their group.

As we'd hoped, when taking our initial draft to focus groups we found that people were able to empathise with characters which bore no relation to their conditions, simply because their emotional realities were so similar regardless of their diagnosis.

THE POWER OF LETTERS

Punctuating the scenes of Hidden Stories you'll find letters written by individuals during, or as a result of, the workshops. These are the direct voices of those people, unedited and left to speak for themselves. They'll relate to the stories you read, but are not meant to be a specific part of any character's narrative.

The letters have been a staple of the workshops and were an important element of an interactive exhibition we ran at Brighton Dome early on in the process. By writing these letters, people were able to have a conversation with what they'd kept hidden, whether a disability, a self-consciousness or an uncertainty. I was deeply touched by what I read in the letters, and by how people spoke to that part of themselves and gained a new perspective by doing so.

I highly recommend writing a letter for yourself; the results could be really enlightening.

Dear Morph-Cloud

You have been with me, within and without for
so long — you are a part of my life. When I was
young you didn't exist for me. When I became
an adult you became me, forever shifting and
melding to form yourself around me.

Sometimes I believe that you are me, that I am
you — that we are inseparable, that we can't
live without each other. Other times I wonder
where or who would I be without you? You are
so very changeable — the days are different
with you, the same patterns appear though like
the weather, the seasons, the movement of my
life. How I long to be free of you, Morph-Cloud
— we have been together for so many years.

If only you would please turn over — I can
learn to live without you. I promise you I can.
I'm giving myself the chance to now, like I
never have before. I can see beyond you,
imagine a life without you. When light shines
through your darkness I can sense another life,
another me.

When you accompany other people (as I'm sure
you do, as I'm sure you will) I will see you,
I will recognise you — I will help others to
do the same, to see you as I do, to know you
as I do, to make our lives without you.
Until that time comes, these words will remain...

M

LET'S KEEP SHARING

Making Hidden Stories truly has been a shared experience for all the participants and supporters involved in its creation. Now we want to share that experience with you.

The book is one story *and* a series of snapshots, so you can read it from beginning to end or drop in wherever you want. You can read it multiple times and possibly discover new things each time you revisit it. You may relate to certain pages or certain characters, while others will offer a window into another person's world.

You may also find that it's a useful tool; a starting point for discussion or a gentler way in to deep or difficult conversations.

Please take whatever you need from it and, when you're done, pass it on. You could give it to a friend or family member, or even a stranger. Drop it into your office, take it to a charity shop or leave it on the bus. You never know who it might find.

It has already been life-changing for some, not least me. Throughout the process I've pushed myself to explore the things I conceal from others, so now I feel I can show more of my own vulnerability and talk about what's going on for me. As a result of being inspired by our amazing participants, I'm starting to live the open and supported life I've always wanted.

Keep in mind this inspiration – and spirit of sharing, empathy and possibility – as the book passes through your hands. Hidden Stories really is about all of us. We all have parts of ourselves we keep hidden; parts we feel others won't understand or that don't seem normal. But we also have the power to rewrite normal.

Now I've shared my journey, I'll leave you to continue yours. I truly hope Hidden Stories helps you, or the people you love, along the way. Lastly, I want to thank everyone who has had the courage to share their stories with us, and in turn with you.

Simon Magnus
Brighton, May 2019

THE STORIES

PART ONE

Meet Anita

Getting ready for work

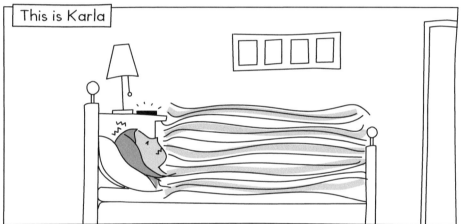

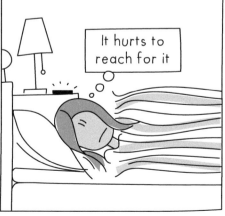

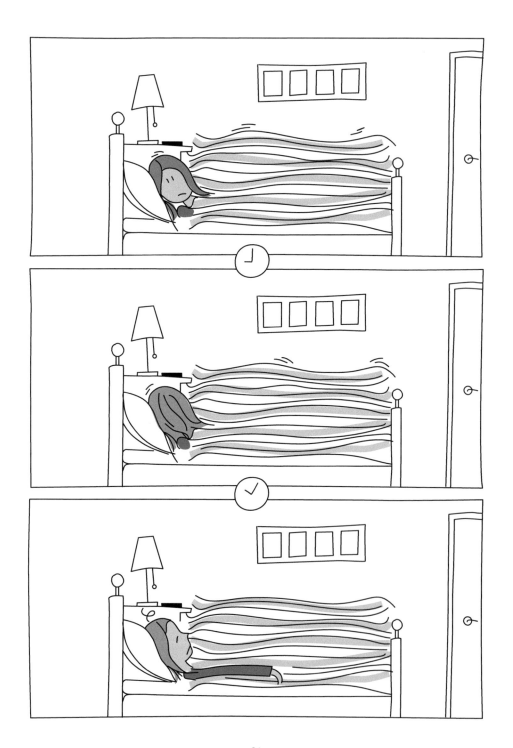

Hello trouble

I see that you are still with me wherever I go. Why? It's hard for me to understand why you can't leave me in peace.

I don't need or want you.

Others don't want me because they confuse me with you. Others judge me for who you are in me and don't take me for who I am. I am not you and you are not me.

Leave my space and my time. I need peace, quiet and no attention.

Thank you in advance

33

Common Contortions

BALLAD OF THE BALL

This is me

[trying to be perfect]

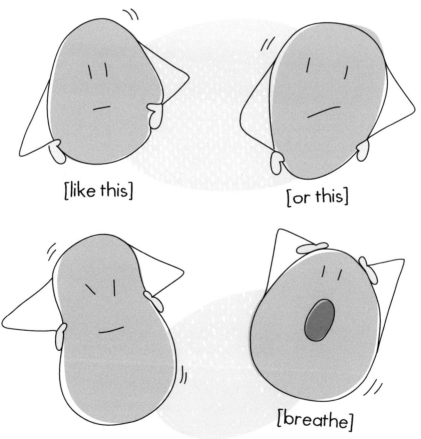

[like this]

[or this]

[breathe]

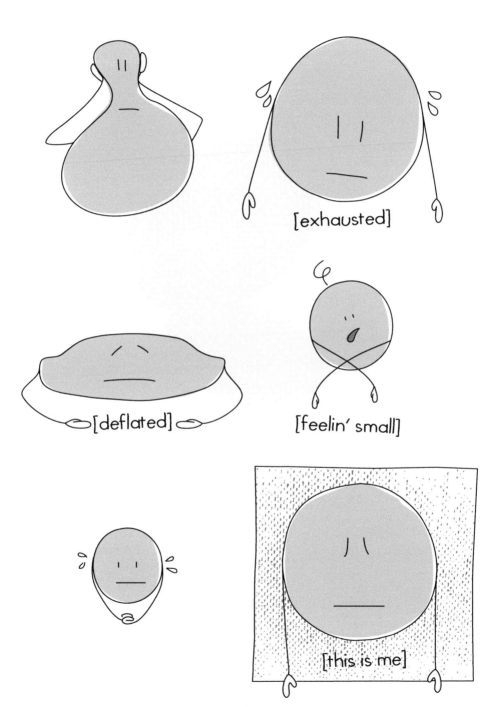

[exhausted]

[deflated]

[feelin' small]

[this is me]

I live in a bit of a fantasy; I like to know what my day is going to bring. If I don't have an itinerary, I might get a bit anxious. You feel you're here but you're not, it's an 'I'm not really here' kind of thing.

If I get onto public transport I get into a fit of giggles or I want to shout out rude words.
I have to really keep that down sometimes because I imagine people in a category; a certain type of person. Keeping all this energy, all these words down all the time.

I visualise things around people. I feel invisible myself, it's a really strange feeling. You're aware you're there, you feel numb, invisible, like it's someone else talking; I'm at the side and another person is doing the talking for me. It's difficult most days. Nodding and smiling in the right places.

For me, normal is just everyone being who they want to be in life. If you're happy and at peace with yourself, to me that's normal.

Voice
from
a crowd

PART TWO

40

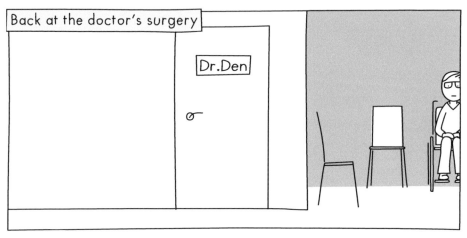

To the panic that erupts

I may have got better at squashing you,
but I suspect you'll always be there.
Sometimes I wonder if you do in fact serve
a purpose: whether you're a warning of
impending danger or a signal that all
is not well.

Mostly, though, I see you as a physical
response to the mental explosions that
people (or the sounds/smells they emit)
cause within me. A sign, for me only,
that it's all too much.

You are a sign that my condition is about
to overwhelm me. And I have to listen or
I'll become 'one of those' people. I look
'normal'; I'm not — but keep that hidden.

Yours knowingly
x

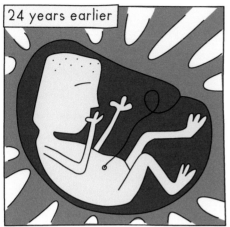

50

Dear Eternal Companion

You almost brought me down but I chose not to be a victim because I would not be here now. It was a difficult process but I AM STILL HERE even though you made me feel like a loser and tried to cause permanent damage to my sight and my balance and my self-esteem.

OK, so the self-esteem is certainly dented but I swam out of the hole you punched in it! I swam through the tunnel of depression; through the mist and around the glass wall into my future where I have adapted and learnt to live with my disabilities, focus on my disabilities and feel immensely grateful for what a good quality of life I have. This does not define who I am or who I may become. I just keep on swimming.

Best wishes,
Your eternal pal

PART THREE

Thank you

I've always ignored that small voice inside me. That inner child who wants to be heard. Who nags for attention.

She's so tired of me telling her to grow up.

Yet here she is with me now, happy that I've listened to what she needs. She was always so worried.

I want to hold her hand. I want to treat her with gentleness, as I would any child.

Why am I always so harsh with her?

I want to show you something

Staff only

Welcome to Planet Not-Normal

Wacky ideas welcome

Earth 32,000 miles

Back on Earth, Karla is still in the park

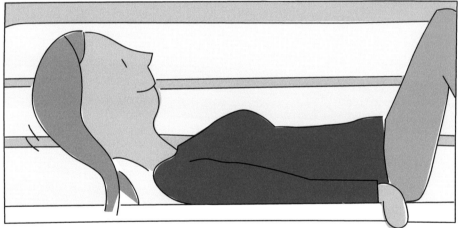

It's time for Anita to come home

TABLE OF CONTENTS

Dear Beloved Within

Don't hide; be truth, explore courageously, for only then will you find that peace you desire. Be free to be you fearlessly, for this pain is only the contraction of holding the truth within.

I will be free, for there is no reason in life to be nothing but true.

Be still, be yourself, be honest, and you will see that you are blessed with a peace within that comes when you release your anxieties. Be proud to be you, expose everything and then liberation will be the wind that blows you freely into a place where you can just be. Know this peace and you will sail freely.

x

to be
continued

'WHEN WE BECOME AWARE
OF THE NUMBER OF PEOPLE
WITH HIDDEN CONDITIONS
MAYBE WE'LL BEGIN
TO QUESTION
WHETHER NORMAL
MEANS ANYTHING AT ALL.'

— ANONYMOUS

AFTERWORD

We took our initial drafts of Hidden Stories to many focus groups, where people living with invisible conditions, and those without, contributed to the evolution of the book.

These people helped us to make more sense of the moments and images we'd created, and bring out people's voices more deeply through the stories we were telling.

Some profound conversations took place as we reviewed Hidden Stories together in these groups. It was extremely interesting to see how people read parts of the book differently. And we also learnt about how best to use it and where to go from there.

We want to share some of these ideas with you. So, carry on reading for a few suggestions on how you can continue your unique journey with Hidden Stories, and to help you share this book with others.

FIRSTLY, OUR BIG INSPIRATION

The intention behind Hidden Stories is to raise awareness of what it's like to live with invisible conditions and to give people more opportunity to connect with others. We were hugely inspired by the people we worked with and also by the work of American social scientist Brené Brown. If you don't know her, make sure you check her out online. Her talks about empathy, vulnerability and shame provided a backbone for the whole project.

SHARED READING

When putting the book together, we felt that what we wanted to say through the images and characters was really clear. But some people in the focus groups interpreted these messages differently; they still found the content meaningful but not necessarily as we'd intended. People have such diverse ways of seeing and sensing the world and nobody will experience things in exactly the same way.

This is OK because we can connect with others, and create understanding, by sharing our individual interpretations of the universe.

Reading is such an individual and personal activity, so it may sound strange to suggest, at the end of a book, that we should try reading it together. But from our own experiences of reading as a group, we feel it's a really worthwhile and interesting experience.

The way you share this book with others will be personal to you and your circumstances. In the focus groups, people suggested using Hidden Stories to connect with loved ones, people who support you (or who you support), health professionals or even work colleagues. If this book is the start of a conversation, what will that mean for you?

One of the amazing things about using images to tell a story is that we're able to convey so much more, to many more people, than if we were using just words. Pictures allow for more open interpretation. So, you can read the lives of the characters in this book from many different angles.

Try sitting down with someone and asking them what they see in Hidden Stories. Their answer might surprise you.

What do you see in the characters and their stories?

What different emotions, thoughts and opinions emerge?

What did you spot that someone else didn't?

What happens when you look at this detail a few more times?

What can you learn about the person (or people) you're reading with by sharing how you feel about the stories?

'DEAR INVISIBLE CONDITION'

Letter-writing has been a big part of Hidden Stories. Since our early work-shops, the idea of addressing letters to what we keep hidden has grown.

Why not try it for yourself? Don't worry about what you'll say. Just start with 'Dear…' then look within, be curious and see what comes next. You might surprise yourself.

You can look at the letters in this book if you want some inspiration, but remember that each person's letter will be individual to them. If you feel comfortable sharing your letter, that could be the start of a new conversation.

WHAT'S IN YOUR LITTLE BOOK OF BEING NORMAL?

Ultimately Hidden Stories is about our own sense of what's normal versus the 'normal' we think we're expected to be.

We hold in our minds an imaginary set of rules on how to be normal. And we put ourselves under pressure to follow these rules, to fit in and be accepted. In Hidden Stories, The Little Book of Being Normal responds to this and calls it out.

Now, imagine creating your own Little Book of Being Normal…

What would your chapter headings be?

What rules do you see all around you that you think are stupid, irrelevant to you or just out of reach?

How would you rewrite those rules?

LAST WORD

If you've been affected by what you've read or seen in this book and don't have anyone you feel comfortable speaking with, give the Samaritans a call for free on 116 123. They're an amazing organisation and have been a life-line for so many people.

To find more Hidden Stories, visit www.hiddenstories.co.uk.

NOTE FROM THE ILLUSTRATOR

ON SELF-COMPASSION

The Hidden Stories project has definitely taught me how to soften my inner-critic and have compassion for my imperfection. Everyone feels inadequate, flawed, and imperfect sometimes. By recognising our common humanity we can begin to move through this.

Like Simon, who I got to know through one of my most compassionate friends, I had never been involved in the creation of a graphic novel. I said yes with enthusiasm and excitement. But when I started to get a notion of the scope of the project (and deadline) — from drawing the initial storyboards to the sketches used as layers for the final digital artwork, through to fine-tuning the emotions of the characters — I found myself in a full-blown panic attack. I froze.

I looked for escape routes and listed all the good reasons why I wasn't the most suitable person to do the job. My inner-critic was shouting out and my body felt tense and in a state of 'flight'.

For a while, my head was an uneasy broth of anxiety and evasive wishful thinking as I feverishly held up my I-can-do-this mask. As with the co-creators, it seemed I was identifying with the stories much more deeply than in the initial sketch phase. Instructions like 'Please draw Mike while hunching near the bench and tying his shoelaces' paralysed me (I was more used to drawing static sheep).

Yet, just by starting — starting where I was — just by taking up my pencil, I softened up and noticed that, step by step, line by line, the storylines of inadequacy and imperfection were dissolving. As my concentration on, and engagement in, the project intensified towards the end, I started to feel enormous gratitude to have been pushed beyond my limits (and self-limiting beliefs) by Simon, and I discovered the self-compassion in saying 'this is good enough'. It might not be perfect but readers do identify with the characters and the feedback we got from the focus groups was overwhelming. It gave me the courage and energy to continue.

There was also a process of letting go, of not clinging to a fixed idea, as many sketches and even some final drawings didn't make it to the book. I learned to sit with 'not holding on'.

To quote Brené Brown: 'Authenticity is a daily choice to show up and be real. The choice to be honest, to let our true selves be seen.' I strongly believe that self-compassion is a gateway to authenticity. By recognising, allowing, investigating and nurturing* my vulnerabilities in this creative process I became more 'real', I became stronger.

Thank you, Simon, for your kindness, authentic enthusiasm and critical yet honest eye. For holding space in moments of doubt and heart-muscle pain. For our Friday 10 o'clock-Skype routine. And, most of all, for being a friend and a compassionate external voice on this journey.

PS – Besides my pencil, my English has been sharpened by many 'new discoveries', like: bay-window, lanyard, destitute, scintillating, plodding, slouched... and many more.

Tinne Luyten
Hasselt (Belgium), May 2019

—

* Referring to the acronym RAIN as introduced by Tara Brach in True Refuge (2013).